LIVING LIFE IN TWO FAITHS

Gregory Rashad

Table of Contents

Preface

This book was written for many reasons. The main reason it was written at the time was because I wanted to sleep! I told my pastor and everybody who would hear it that I was going to write a book about why I reverted back to Christianity. I spoke of it for years, but I had never put pen to paper to get the process going. I thought when I got time, I would finally get to write this book. I started writing the book a couple of years ago but got too busy to finish. Now that I have retired, it is time to get out my memoir about God's grace and mercy towards my family and me.

Now I know many times when I would hear people say that God had spoken to them, I would think these people are crazy. I still have doubts about certain people who say this but as for myself, God spoke to me as clear as day. Believe it or not, I really don't care but I now understand when you have the Holy Ghost, God wants your attention at strange hours of the day. A lot of times it is when everybody is asleep because that is the one time He can get your undivided attention. I would hear my name called out just like a friend would call out your name to get your attention. The problem with this was that I would be dead asleep! God would get my attention and I was never able to ignore it and go back to sleep. No matter how much medication I had taken to get me back to sleep, after hearing His voice, I would be wide awake. I either humbly listened to what He was trying to tell me, or I would just watch television until my wife woke up for work and talk to her until she left. I usually would be in a bad mood the rest of the day because once I finally got tired enough to sleep, the kids would wake up and be raring to go. One morning I heard my name called and finally I was like, "Lord, if you let me get some rest, I will write the book and start telling people about Your goodness. I will do whatever it takes to get Your Word out and not on my time." I knew it would be a hard task because a lot of stuff about Islam I had completely forgot about. When the Lord gives you freedom from something, you don't really take time out to reflect on the bad stuff. I know I owed God, and this was just a sample of what I am sure He is going to want me to do. I am thankful that even through all the years I was in Islam and never gave Jesus Christ His just due or respect that all mankind should give Him; He kept me. He kept me from harm, death or any other thing imaginable so that one day I would be able to say that Jesus is Lord. He is the beginning and the end, Alpha and Omega, and I will praise Him the rest of my life. My Lord, my God, here is my testimony of Your mercy and grace.

Islam and Christianity
Living Life in the Two Abrahamic Faiths

———————— ❧ ————————

Why did you convert to the religion of Islam and then revert back to Christianity? I think I have been asked this question a thousand times. It had nothing to do with recent or past terrorist attacks or anything like that. It has been jokingly said that those instances are the reasons I reverted back, but I would hope people know me well enough to know that I don't take my faith lightly. It is literally a life and death situation. That is nothing to play with. It was strictly true doctrine that took a while longer to be revealed to me because of my ignorance and a very hard head. I was never associated with anyone who wanted to cause harm to America. In fact, when I used to go to the mosque/masjid in Richmond, Virginia, I went with people who proudly served our Armed Forces. To be truthful, a lot of the Muslims I associated with were American born. Some were African American who grew up in Islamic doctrine either through Sunni Islam or the Nation of Islam.

When the question arose about my conversion and subsequent reversion, there was only one answer I could give them. I saw something in the Bible that scared me to death! It wasn't like it was something that just popped in the Bible. Of course, it had been there the whole time, but some people have to understand and receive revelation at different times in their life. I understand now that pastors have a very hard job. They have to be able to receive revelation and discern biblical principles, not man's principles. There are hidden gems in the Bible that a person will only be able to understand through divine revelation. They have to piece this together through different scriptures to give a message that people will understand. I say piece scriptures together because every word in the Bible must agree from Genesis to Revelation. The whole Bible must agree, or His Word wouldn't be true.

The congregation will now have the information to study for themselves and they will have to discern if the pastor's word is from God or from the pastor. I assure you if it is from the pastors, it won't be true, but if it is from God, the Word will bear fruit. What scared me I will get to later in this book, but I do know it was the best decision of my life and I know without a shadow of a doubt that even though I was not on the path designed for me by God, Jesus watched over me. When I was in my confusion searching for Him, He truly blessed me when I accepted Him as my Lord and Savior. In hindsight, maybe it was the path for me so I would be able to give my testimony of how God saved me, and I would be better able to spread the message of Jesus to those who are in similar situations and give Him all the glory.

Before I go any further with my story, I want to put a disclaimer out there so people will better understand what I am trying to say. I, in no way, am making fun of or discrediting or condemning anybody's race or religion. I am telling a truthful story about things I have personally experienced and my feelings AT THAT TIME on certain issues. I have evolved and my thoughts and actions are not the same as they were 25 years ago. I know if some people read this, they will say, "I knew he was racist." That is not true, and I never was racist, I was hurt and hurt can make you say and think some ignorant things especially if you don't let God flow through you. I have religious tolerance of all religions and will be the first one to defend your right to practice the faith however you like. I am not a doctor or scholar of philosophical doctrine on religions of the world. I just want you to know what I personally know to be true because of the Holy Ghost within me that guides me daily. My Holy Ghost is better than any degree you may be able to attain and I will dispute that fact with anyone who would dare to argue. You can have all the degrees you want, but that doesn't mean you are called to get in a pulpit and preach the gospel to me or anyone else. Some of the best pastors I have encountered have had nothing more than a high school education. They might have gone back for more education on religious studies, but it is hard to beat the Holy Ghost which is God in us, and we are sure to receive it because God doesn't lie. It was promised to all of us in Acts; 2, 38 where it reads, "Then Peter said unto them, Repent, and be baptized every one of you in the name of Jesus Christ for the remission of sins, and ye shall receive the gift of the Holy Ghost." I don't want anybody out here thinking I am condemning a certain religious or racial group. I went through many transformations to find the truth and some people may believe that what is truth to me is not really their truth. I pray for you on your journey for truth and pray that God helps you to realize that He is the only one who can comfort us and show us who He really is. Once you ask God to show you, you will be amazed at how enlightened you will become. Believe me when I tell you, He showed Himself many times and He was there the whole time, and I just didn't see Him. I only discuss how good God is and on that, we can all agree!

Marion, Virginia aka Small-Town America!

I grew up in a little town in Southwest, Virginia. Marion, Virginia was the place I reluctantly called home. I always wanted to be in the city and craved city life; I still do to this day. I would move to almost any city on the east coast and some Midwestern cities if my wife gave me permission, but she grew up in Far Rockaway Queens, New York and would rather not have to deal with that grind everyday much less raise our kids in that environment. Marion was a quaint little town known for being the home of Hungry Mother State Park, Brunswick, Southwestern Virginia Mental Health Institute and the famous soft drink, Mountain Dew. Other than that, there isn't much else happening in Marion. When I was growing up, the population was approximately 7,500 people and state agencies and factory workers dominated the area. The thing that always disturbed me was that Marion was at a minimum 93% white! Most of the blacks lived in two different parts of town and I knew most of them at the time. I lived on the infamous Iron Street (AKA Needmore Street, nicknamed Needmore because most of the people on that street just needed more)! Everybody knew this street even if you were white and weren't selling drugs or you were really talented in sports and played at the recreation center or later on in life at Steele Park named in honor of one of my uncles William (Bill) Steele. This might not have been the best place for you to be unless you just happened to be some of the few poor or working-class people that lived there. I was told by some of the older guys in the neighborhood that if we ever got into trouble with white people and could just get back to the recreation department that was located on the corner of Iron Street, we were good to go! Who knows if that was true or not, but I do know when I was young, Needmore was my safe haven. Back then, we were allowed to roam and play all up and down Iron Street. We all rolled in packs. I couldn't imagine letting my own kids do that now because people have changed over the years and so has Iron Street. It's sad because my kids will never have the freedom of enjoying friends and the street like we did as kids. I do know because some of the kids told me that they didn't feel comfortable on Iron Street and not many people who weren't from there dared to cross that invisible barrier. Only the kids who were from surrounding neighborhoods played at the rec and the field.

Growing up, I don't remember race being an issue while I was young coming up through primary and elementary schools. It was once that I got to junior high that I could tell some of the kids were going to continue to be cool because we were in the same socioeconomic class or we had just been cool for years and their parents taught them to look at the person inside instead of the outside appearance. Unfortunately, there were too few cases like that with the kids I grew up with. The others I noticed later on in life because we just stopped talking to each other. It wasn't that we stopped talking to each other over a beef or argument. Maybe it was because they noticed that I wasn't at the Country Club with them and their families socializing every weekend playing golf or at the pool. Sports kept some of my friends active with me because we always played sports on the streets of our neighborhood or participated through school. I do remember a kid that I was really cool with in junior high said the word nigger speaking about another friend of mine. Once he realized that he made the statement in front of me, he tried to explain to me that the person he was referring to had "nigger qualities" and that he didn't think that way about all "colored people." From that day as a young man growing up in Marion, Virginia, I became very uncomfortable in my own skin. You could not try to be like them because frankly I come from a single parent household; my mother was working sometimes two jobs and working on various boards in the community and we did not have the finances to do what the other middle income white people were doing. (Just a side note that my mother had the energy to do that. Raising a knucklehead like me is amazing to me and I have to admire and love that quality in her. As I raise my kids now, I know that was not an easy task. I just want to thank her for everything she has done and still does for me. I love you, Jenny)! Now God forbid in my neighborhood you try to act white or socialize with the so-called country clubbers, the characters on our street would have punished you. I would have to act more ignorant than I am sometimes because if you dared say you wanted to go to college and make something of yourself, because of the crab in a barrel mentality that a lot of black people have, I would have caught hell from both sides and that is a lot of stress to a young black man coming up in small-town America. I don't want to bore you with these trivial details of my life that don't have anything to do with the testimony and blessing I am trying to portray to you, but I want you to understand my backstory a little bit because that way you can see how life has affected the certain roads taken in life. My backstory shows how my environment did awaken me to certain social norms that were going on at the time that should not have been acceptable anywhere. The backstory sets up my reasoning for looking to Islam for some type of peace and pride about me and my people. Unfortunately, we still have these norms in towns like where I live but don't think that it is not happening in more urban areas as well. The outright racism and bigotry in bigger cities and even on social media are making national headlines daily. It just wasn't as openly expressed in these areas until we had a black man to run for president and WIN! Our 2016 presidential election or catastrophe (whichever you want to call it) really brought out people's true colors. I say that because on social media and news outlets everywhere, it really became an us-against-them attitude. One candidate even took his time to denounce the endorsement of David Duke and the Ku Klux Klan by lying and saying he knew nothing about him. The Alt-Right group which is a racist/separatists group stood by and endorsed this candidate. People came out in droves to vote for this candidate who lost the popular vote but won the Electoral College by a good margin. Republican or Democrat, I believe the election was fueled by one reason, RACE! It wasn't white against black in the elections, but it might as well have been. A rural part of the country did not want a woman to carry on the policies of a black man who was presently in office. People came out of the woodworks to make sure that did not happen. On a personal level, I am happy that in 2020, America elected someone who will try to bring some common ground on the race issue, but I fear that this country is as divided as I have ever seen it and the next president will have a tough job ahead of him. On January 6, 2020, we had an assault on our democracy at the Capitol building. One of the worst days in American history and I believe it was partly a race issue.

On social media, I saw an ugly side of people I grew up with that I consider friends that I had never seen before and it made me question if they were truly friends. What did they really think about me and my family? Needless to say, I did a lot of unfollowing on my social media accounts because I couldn't stand to read what they were saying about

America's politics. It had a hint of racism in every word or they were just ignorant of the truth of racism. I have yet to figure that out. People of my own age group in my community still refer to black people as colored or call a grown black man boy. It is amazing to me that even until this day black folk are still referred to in these terms by white people who really don't understand how offensive these terms are. I went through school and tolerated it because they didn't put their hands on me. They could say anything they wanted but as long as they didn't cross that line, they wouldn't hear a word from me. Please believe I have never forgotten those words though. Those are the things that sting even into adulthood and you can either shake it off and keep praising God for just being there and giving you the patience to endure it, or you can let that hurt shape and mold you and keep an empty feeling that will shape you and you realize you have become something outside of God's will. Unfortunately, I chose the latter and had to pay the consequences for it later. BUT I HAVE BEEN REDEEMED!

College Years and Enlightenment!

As I got older in college and hung out with the brothas from bigger cities and watched how they carried themselves, I questioned why I would want to demean myself and think less of myself just because of what I saw and heard in Small-town America. I was better than that and I was looking for something or someone to help me assert myself and become prideful of my rich heritage and culture without wincing as I often did if someone mentioned black people in class (I still do to this day occasionally). I got really tired of that and wanted something better for myself and future family. Once I left Marion, I was never coming back! Mentally, I had left Marion years ago and couldn't stand the thought of living in small-town America again. Only thing that was good to me about Marion was the Job Corps Center for all the women who went to the center and the few family members that remained. Most of my family and a lot of blacks in general left years ago and never looked back. As I read this I am thinking how God has made a liar out of me! I am sure He will continue to if I make plans without consulting Him first. (Sometimes we never learn)! I started reading books and biographies on W.E.B Dubois and Frederick Douglass but there was one book that really caught my attention and it really did change my life, and a lot of people say my religion for a brief time and period. The Autobiography of Malcolm X is one of the most riveting books I have ever read in my life besides the King James Version of the Bible. I could understand the wounds that Malcolm carried around with him until the day he died because, I too, had heard such foul things come out of white people's mouth and I came to the conclusion that they didn't want to be around me so in my mind, screw them! I didn't want to be around any of those REDNECK CRACKERS either. Was that the right disposition to take? Of course not, but as far as I was concerned, I was done with white people and except for a select few that I just could not turn on. I mostly stayed in my own neighborhood and around my own people. Without fully understanding what Malcolm was trying to say in his autobiography at the end, I started listening to an energetic black man who would call the white man a devil to his face. He would also show how the white man was deceptive to the black man by using the government as its cover. I also listened to Minister Louis Farrakhan who was an eloquent speaker and still is. The thing that caught my attention about these two men was their bravery for calling white people out and telling them how they really felt about the plight of the black man in America. They were telling black men to clean yourselves up, get off drugs and take care of your families. Look like the black king and queen you were. They were rougher on black people than you could ever imagine because they were trying to instill discipline in black folks that most were not used to. They were also using God as their vessel to clean these young men up and anytime you include God in your undertakings, that had to be a good thing, right?

I should name this book **"Be careful what you listen to."** I went and dug up all the information I could with a close friend of mine. We read any and all information we could get on Malcolm X and Minister Farrakhan. My friend's mother was **very pro black.** She was the only person I had seen for years brave enough to wear African apparel and keep her afro! She was smart and educated like my mother and she would be quick to tell you to know yourself and educate yourself so you can survive in this society. My friend and I would look up all this information and you have to understand that was hard for us in small-town Marion because a lot of people, especially black people, didn't know anything about either of these men. I don't remember one history teacher in public school teaching anything about Malcolm X or Minister Farrakhan. Libraries weren't running over with information about them and there was no Wikipedia in those days, so we actually had to do the research. Young kids today would have had a stroke if they had to do the work we did gathering any data we could on these two enigmatic leaders because the hard copy resources just were not available. The thing that I really noticed and stuck out to me was in their religion, Allah (God) was one person, not a triune god.

I grew up in a Methodist church which believes in the trinity and the way I understood it, the trinity meant that there were three (3) entities which formed one (1) God. I'm far from a mathematician but that just didn't add up to me. The church that I went to had an enormous history with African Americans in our community, but I never felt at home or at peace in that church. The church had so many ceremonies and rituals. The preachers spoke of God's love for humanity but never explained that God had another side to Him that

He couldn't stand about humans which was sin that could have us awaken to HELL. I never remember sin being a central topic, but I heard a lot about love. Don't get me wrong – I know God loves us, but I am also aware He despises our sinful ways. It appeared to me the truth was dumbed down because if the preacher was too rough, they would throw him out and get another one they liked. In the short 18 years I went to the Methodist church, we had at least six different pastors. I remember quoting the Apostles Creed every week. There is a part in there that states, "I believe in the Holy Catholic Church." Why did we believe in the Catholic church? That seemed odd to me until after much study I saw how much the Catholic church had tainted most protestant churches around the world to what they wanted the masses to know. Why is the Catholic church hiding the truth and what are they hiding? These were questions I always wanted to know but never really got the answers I wanted. Our church had many more problems than that though. To me the problem was that the older members thought of us as a burden and really didn't want to be bothered with the kids. My mom and another lady were our Sunday school teachers, and they were really good at teaching us about God, but it just appeared that any activity that they wanted to do with the youth was frowned upon especially if it came to money. (Just side notes: if you don't want to see your church doors close for good, invest in the youth because they are the ones who will keep those doors open in the future). I later learned after the youth had left the church and the church itself was on the brink of closing because of lack of membership that a lot of the things the youth did get to do was funded by the other Sunday school teacher's father who contributed a lot to youth activities. I later started going to a Pentecostal church in my neighborhood. I really started learning that Jesus was God who wrapped Himself in flesh to come into the world to die on the cross and save us from eternal damnation. There was no trinity spoken of here because God was and still is a jealous God and there could only be one (1). God had many titles but once He came and died for our sins, we didn't need a mediator. We could call Him by His name which is Jesus. We as a people have titles like husband, brother; daddy etc… but we all have a name! The way that was broken down in its simplicity by my current pastor just amazed me. Don't think that I wasn't taught and showed what Jesus was about at an early age. A bishop and his late wife whom I actually love and adore took time out of their days to show me my walk with Christ, but I just didn't get it at the time. I would have probably stayed at that church but a lady who was a member asked me one day, "When are you gonna get away from them old Methodists and Baptists?" That let me know at the time that she looked down on others for how they practiced their faith, and I didn't want to be a part of that. Word to the wise – if someone comes into the faith and they are new, be careful how you talk to them because words can have them run away, not from God, but from you!

Sometimes immaturity can blind you to the truth, but I couldn't grasp or understand the trinity. It just never made sense to me how three (3) different entities could form one (1) God especially if God was a jealous God. I had a hard time with the Pentecostal church in my neighborhood because they had a lot of rules that didn't make sense to me and I did not see the rules as being biblical. No makeup for women and they had to wear plain looking dresses or skirts every day to show modesty. I'm sorry and maybe I am a feminist, but a woman can be modest in a pair of jeans, just my opinion. You couldn't listen to secular music which would not have worked for me. I love any and all kinds of music except country and listening to James Cleveland and a few of the gospel singers that my mom would kick me out of the house for on Sundays. They would have given me a headache so that couldn't happen. Even with all of this teaching, it just got to the point that I saw no need to go to church. I was very confused about biblical principles. In mom's house, you went to church until you were of age and then you had a choice. You had to hear the guilt about not giving God a little bit of your time each week because you gave the devil all of your time partying and running up and down the street chasing women. I knew I wasn't going to step foot in the church she went to ever again and I didn't want to go to the church on my street because they would pester you to get the Holy Ghost. If you have never tarried with an Elder to receive the Holy Ghost, you don't know trauma. It was really almost traumatizing but now that I have it, it seems so simple to receive. I was just a hard- headed young man who thought that with some reading of my own and philosophical teaching by religious scholars, it would give me all the answers that I needed. This Islam I was reading about had really piqued my interest. It didn't seem as rule-bearing as Christianity appeared to be at the time. As a young person, fewer rules were exactly what I was looking for! What a fool I was!

El Hajj Malik El Shabazz

I had left college for a while vowing to get my degree later. It was like a family thing that you had to get that degree because education was the one thing people could never take from you. (Good Lord, I can still hear my mother telling me all that jazz about getting a good education). I had other things going on and I was basically lost inside and out. Reading on the Nation of Islam or NOI for a short period of time occupied my time and led me to believe that was what I wanted to be, a MUSLIM. First things first though, pork and alcohol had to go, even weed! I had no problems giving up weed and alcohol wasn't my vice. Women were my vice. Now about those foods! I was going to have to give up chitlins, pigs feet, salted pork, pork chops, ham hocks, sausage, spare ribs, and bacon. **What in the world am I gonna eat?** You never realize how bad your diet might be until you take away a major food group! I have weighed over 300 pounds for most of my youth and adult life. I had been used to a bad diet. We ate cheap and I ate a lot. Sometimes when my kids are eating me out of house and home at the age of eight years old, I now understand my mother's struggle of trying to feed me. I had a hard time at first trying to find substitutes for these items but once I moved away from small-town, I realized that sometimes even Christians gave up these foods and had to look for alternatives. I figured heart disease runs in my family; it couldn't hurt to eat a little more turkey and turkey alternatives. These were things I was going to have to discipline myself with because if I wanted to be proud and be able to pass on good information and habits to my kids, I had to be disciplined myself. A certain book I was reading at the time was "The Autobiography of Malcolm X" transcribed by Alex Haley. Haley was a brilliant author in his own right winning acclaim back in the 70's with his own family tree written in book form called "Roots" and having a major miniseries named after the book which I am sure made America take a look at itself. I am sure America did not like what it saw because it made America look like a bunch of savages. Funny story – I remember trying to watch Roots as a child with my grandmother and mother when I was only five or six. I remember them cutting off Kunta Kinte's foot. His role was played by John Amos. John Amos was the stern father "James" on the sitcom "Good Times." I thought to myself that if they cut off James' foot, I can't watch or imagine what they do to everybody else! I went to my room and played Pong because I didn't want to see any more of that movie. I was actually a grown man when I completed watching the series with my wife. (I was such an ignorant child). Malcolm was the epitome of discipline with help from The Honorable Elijah Muhammad. Malcolm cleaned himself up, got off drugs, and wanted to use his temple to get the word out about Allah. I thought that this was the person I needed to try and emulate to reach the goal of self-fulfillment. I was going to model myself after a man who was a former pimp and hustler, clean myself up, and live a righteous life.

Malcolm X, born Malcolm Little in Omaha, Nebraska, a man whose name is tattooed on my right arm to this day, is a very controversial figure in America but actually was adored abroad because of his Pan Africanism philosophy. Most know him as a militant black man who called white people blue-eyed devils and told black men to take their rights as a human being "by any means necessary." People have tried to come up with their own ideology of what he really meant by that statement and this I can guarantee you – they were wrong. Not one time did Malcolm X ever express his desire for an uprising of the black race against the white race. In fact, he was quite fond of and very friendly with Mike Wallace of CBS news. What Malcolm could not stand to see was black men on the streets getting attacked by the police with water hoses and dogs. Black folk were getting killed down south and nobody was arrested or even charged for the crimes against the black man. (Sound familiar? It's still happening today. WAKE UP, PEOPLE!) He along with advice from his mentor, The Honorable Elijah Muhammad, devised a plan that would help solve the problem for the time. His philosophy was complete separation of the black man and the white man. Since the black man had a hand in building this country, give the black man a third of the country to govern and police for themselves and the white man could have the rest. This would all but eliminate all of the brutality in the country against brown-skinned people. Even in 1993, I could get with that plan. I had seen enough bigotry and hate in small-town to see that was a good solution. Malcolm X preached this for years and considered other civil rights leaders Uncle Toms for marching and sit-ins just to get whipped by the police. It made no sense to him and it doesn't make any sense to me now as a grown man. There was no way that Malcolm X and Dr. Martin Luther King could have ever worked together in those conditions. Malcolm didn't want to fit in, he just wanted to pack up and go to his own land away from the oppression. He wanted the black man to become the kings and queens we once were before we were stripped from our land and religion. That is hardly a militant stance. What he was teaching in the late 50's and early 60's resonated with me. What really intrigued me was once Malcolm X exposed his mentor of being a drunkard and womanizer, his own people that he stood up for and would have gone through Hell with gasoline drawers on, turned on him. I am intrigued because reading his autobiography we see how Malcolm evolved. Sometimes what we think is a bad thing is later used for His good to praise his Holy name. They suspended Malcolm from the Nation of Islam and he made a quest to Mecca for a pilgrimage which is supposed to be made by any Muslim at least once in their lifetime if they are financially able. Malcolm finally understood what true Islam was all about during his pilgrimage because he ate, slept and prayed with people who had blue eyes, blond hair that he had previously called a devil. They did not look at his outward appearance but the fact that he was there to worship God just as he was. This had a profound effect on Malcolm once he returned and this is why I admire the man to this day. He realized that he was wrong in condemning a race of people because of the cowardly acts that were perpetrated against the black man in America. Malcolm was evolving and embracing the change in thinking better than most of us do in our lifetime. We are usually more resistant to change but Malcolm showed me how you see the wrong, you must correct it and move on. He became a Sunni Muslim, changed his name to EL Hajj Malik EL Shabazz and renounced the teachings of the Honorable Elijah Muhammad. He started an outreach organization to help disenfranchised black people called The Organization of Afro American Unity and Muslim Mosque Inc. He was beginning to get traction to go to the United Nations to file charges against the United States for Crimes against Humanity for the atrocities that were placed on black people throughout the years. He stated he would work with other civil rights groups to help people out, even white people. His only clause, white people could not join his organization because black people first had to learn to do it for self. (It's a shame that black people still have not learned to do it for themselves). He did not want black people subject to what white people thought was the best idea for them such as groups like the NAACP did at the time. Once he came back to the United States and his view changed, he now became a threat. He thought that if people learned the true meaning and practices of Islam we could have harmony amongst the races; true Islam was the only viable option to cure the ails of our countries' racism. He was a threat to the Nation of Islam because he would expose its leaders for who they were and he became a threat to the United States because in my opinion, Malcolm was a very moral man. Unlike Dr. King, the FBI had a lot of information about Dr. King and his extra-marital affairs were prepared to use it against him. I believe that did curtail a little bit of Dr. King's effectiveness to help black people at the time. Malcolm would be better enabled to organize black men to stand up for themselves because he did not have those things hanging over his head. In my honest opinion and after hearing the comedian Dick Gregory give testimony on the autopsy report, the Nation of Islam was blamed for killing Malcolm X. A few members might have had their part in the assassination but the Federal government with information from J. Edgar Hoover killed Malcolm X. If you ever get a chance, watch Dick Gregory's account of the murder and autopsy report. It will make you think that maybe

Minister Farrakhan is right, the government assassinated people who they could not control. Dr. King, even with all of the wiretaps and surveillance they had on him, could have derailed anything he wanted to do but could not stop his voice or movement. He had to go! Malcolm held on strong to principles and was a Godly man who once barked a lot and shocked the masses with his rhetoric, now spoke quietly and spoke with such sternness, they knew Malcolm X also had to go. Imagine what could have happened if the two joined forces and worked together. Malcolm died at the age of 39, the same age of Dr. King at his death. Malcolm had so much to give but the truth killed him. Who is still up for debate, but one thing remains is his teachings still have a deep influence on me of what a man is supposed to be and I pray my children truly understand what he was truly about. As Ossie Davis remembered Malcolm at his eulogy, "Malcolm was our shining black prince who didn't hesitate to die because he loved us so."

Minister Louis Farrakhan and The Nation of Islam

Now if you want to talk about controversy, Minister Farrakhan is the epitome of controversy. I have heard him called anti-Semitic, racist, homophobic and any other negative adjective you can think of used to describe this man. The thing that always caught my attention about Minister Farrakhan was that he is a very eloquent speaker. My mother would have called him a silver-tongued devil; he is very smooth and persuasive with arguments and philosophies about what is going on in the world. Minister Louis X, as he was called at the time, was a minister in the Nation of Islam who was deeply devoted to the teachings of the Honorable Elijah Muhammad and Malcolm X. Louis X took over New York mosque #7 in Harlem that was at one time Malcolm X's mosque. Once Malcolm X was suspended from the Nation of Islam, Louis X took over and became very bitter against Malcolm X. Later it was thought that Minister

Farrakhan had possibly had a personal hand in the assassination of Malcolm X because of his inflammatory rhetoric towards Malcolm and his family about the assassination. Don't think that he was the only one; the famous Muhammad Ali who was a close personal friend of Malcolm's also turned his back on Malcolm X and stated he deserved to die for lying about a prophet (Elijah Muhammad). I believe later in life Muhammad Ali later regretted that stance. Minister Farrakhan advanced in the Nation of Islam until Elijah Muhammad's death in 1974. Elijah Muhammad's son, Warith Deen Muhammad, took over as leader of the Nation of Islam, but he took the organization into a different direction. Warith Deen took the in the direction of orthodox Islam or Sunni Islam. I was later a part of that organization when I joined in 1993 in Durham, North Carolina. Minister Farrakhan initially made the move with Warith Deen Muhammad and embraced Sunni Islam which he actually still practices to this day. For some odd reason, maybe it was for power. but Farrakhan left that organization and revitalized the Nation of Islam in 1981. He opened up over 130 mosques that had been closed and bought back all the properties that were previously owned by the Nation of Islam including the famous mosque in

Chicago, Mosque Maryam. Because of his statements dealing with race, he made the Nation of Islam relevant again in the inner cities with the black youth. Farrakhan and the Nation once again were telling black people to awaken to the atrocities that were happening all over America. Just because the same degree of lynchings and killings weren't as prevalent in the 80's as they were in the 60's, our government found a new way to kill black America, crack cocaine hit the inner cities hard during the early eighties. Alcohol had continuously done its job with black men, but we were under a new strain of attack from our government. There have always been rumors of the CIA planting crack cocaine in our inner cities and even today it was hard for me to object to the idea with the information we have now. That is one of the things I loved about Farrakhan, he too would call anyone out who he thought oppressed our brothers and sisters. This type of so-called militant rhetoric and admonishment from a man of my own skin tone was exactly what I was looking for. I only had one problem with Farrakhan and the Nation of Islam; they had a belief at the time that a mad scientist named Yacub created the white race and that was the reason for their pale dog-like skin as they called it and stringy hair. At that particular time, I hate to say but I was calling white girls cave bitches because of some of the Nation's rhetoric and a rapper who is a member of the Nation of Islam (Ice Cube) made the statement in one of his songs. This all stemmed from Yacub, also a man named Master Fard Muhammad came to Detroit and taught Elijah Muhammad everything about the religion and blessed him to be the prophet and go retrieve the Lost tribe of Shabazz (the black man). Let me also state as a sidebar that there is not nor ever was a tribe of Shabazz in Africa. Master Fard Muhammad was God incarnate! He is responsible for poisoning Islam in the United States among black people as far as I'm concerned, and they fell for it hook line and sinker.

As stated earlier I believe Farrakhan to be an eloquent speaker because he is so charismatic and smooth when he speaks. However, I must warn all Christian elders, pastors and bishops; Farrakhan can preach Jesus as good as you can! If you don't believe me look at some of his sermons on YouTube. I have heard Farrakhan say that "I am a Jesus freak!" He is not saying this only at mosques around the country, he is stating this in churches where he is invited to speak. He is fishing for followers in the churches and anywhere else he can get them preaching about Jesus but is slick and sly when speaking about the prophet Muhammad or Elijah Muhammad. By the time you realize it you are going to mosques and listening to him because he has a lot of truth in him. I still listen to him when he speaks on world events or politics because he is usually telling the truth. Let me state here that I do not in any way believe that Farrakhan is trying to deceive anybody. Islam is his faith and what he tells you is what was taught to him and he wants to stay out of Hell. I truly believe that, but we have many people who have the Word unfortunately twisted; let's hope one day Jesus shows them the truth before it's too late. I know he knows God's Word because he usually preaches from The Holy Bible and The Holy Quran. The problem with teaching out of the Bible for him from my viewpoint, he doesn't have the Holy Ghost to give him revelation or discernment of the true meaning of the Bible.

Even though I had great interest in the Nation of Islam, there was one area we disagreed; I did not believe all white people were the devil. Sure, there were some who acted like that, but I knew black people who once they got that drink in them, I swore they were the devil. I had a few friends that I wondered how I could look in the eye and say that I was a member of a religious organization and we thought the

WHITE man was the devil. In my good conscious I could not fathom such an idea. I will not name the friends who made me realize that the Nation of Islam was not for me, but you probably know who you are because we are good friends to this day. For that, I want to thank you for keeping me true to myself and not trying to be a racist that I knew I wasn't. Thank you from the bottom of my heart!

Warith Deen Muhammad

This will be a short section because this man, Warith Deen Muhammad, was a peaceful man who was not really known except for the fact that he was Elijah Muhammad's son but what some don't know is that he is the one who told Malcolm X of his father's infidelities. He exposed his father to Malcolm and once Malcolm said something, he was killed for it. Warith Deen Muhammad served a prison term at the insistence of his father instead of just doing community service due to failing to enlist in the military. Warith Deen Muhammad knew true Islam and knew when he took over the NOI that he would be personally responsible for the conversion of two million NOI members to orthodox/Sunni Islam. His focus was on being racially inclusive and stressing cooperation between multiple faiths. He was a simple man who had his headquarters in Charlotte, North Carolina, never had an entourage following him; he just wanted to teach about Allah and his prophet Muhammad. Once I started following Warith Deen

Muhammad's teaching and understanding Sunni Islam, I could not wait to join this organization. He taught as Islam speaks of the oneness of God that made absolute sense to me. This was what I was going to be! I was going to be a Muslim! Let me say here there are rules or things that we must abide by once we follow a particular denomination, but people really do not understand or know Islam until they really get into it. Only thing I can say is wow! It was an eye opener because there are so many laws and traditions I believe it is absolutely impossible to follow them all. Before I hear anyone else complaining about Muslims not condemning radical Islam or its attacks, this man was one of the first to denounce the terrorists' attacks on September 11, 2001. Funny how nobody ever hears about this, but he wanted to present Islam as it is truly meant to be, a peaceful religion. Just to end this section I want to say rest in peace to Warith Deen Muhammad because under his teaching of Islam I did grow as a man and probably would not be the man I am without the discipline that was instilled in me from his teachings and the religion of Islam if I were to be truthful.

My Journey into Islam

I remember the day. I had just recently moved to Durham North Carolina and I was staying with a friend's aunt at the time. He and I were going to start going back to college at NC Central and start life out in Tar Heel country while doing everything possible to stay out of Marion, Virginia. We didn't live far from campus so while riding around campus one day, I noticed a mosque right across from the football field. I told my friend I was going to drop him off at the house and I was going to the mosque and check it out. While there I got a chance to profess my Shahada which is a statement of faith. Afterwards it was time for prayer, so I got to pray with the brothers at the mosque and I stayed there for quite a while. I thought that was one of the happiest days of my life. Muslims don't baptize but they do have something called ablution which is basically taking a shower. The imam told me that in order to finish this process at home that I needed to take a shower and show that I was new in Allah and to be purified from the world. What is really crazy about this whole situation is that once I got out the shower, I went straight to the strip club! I had supposedly washed all my sins away, but I couldn't get away from them strip clubs. Women were always a weakness for me. I just loved women but in hindsight this was absolutely ridiculous. I bet the Imam didn't mean for me to do that. At least I didn't drink or eat swine, so I was good at the strip club! What a ridiculous mindset I had at the time!

Let me be clear that just because I professed my Shahada (profession of faith), don't think I didn't have quite a bit to learn. Let me give you a very brief synopsis of Islam.

Five (5) Pillars of Islam are:

1. Shahada - Profession of faith - "There is no God, but Allah and Prophet Muhammad is his messenger.
2. Salat - Prayers made five times daily.
3. Zakat - Charity given each year based on the individual's accumulated wealth.
4. Sawm – Fasting during the month of Ramadan which lasts approximately 28-30 days.
5. Hajj – Pilgrimage to Mecca to be completed once

in a lifetime by every Muslim.

Articles of Faith are:

1. Belief in God! It states in Sura 112, ayat's 1-4 of the Holy Quran "Say He is God, the one and only, God, the Eternal, Absolute, He begetteth not, nor is begotten: And there is none like unto Him." Muslims reject the trinity and divinity of Jesus and believe there is no need for intermediaries.

2. Belief in Angels – They worship God in total obedience. They record actions, glorify God and take souls at the time of death. Jinn – Made of fire and evil, invisible to all humans. Satan's or Shaitans are the devil's armies which are here to go against the will of God. Islam does not believe that Shaitan is a fallen angel. They believe he is Jinn because angels have no authority or will to do anything but praise and worship God.

3. Revelations – Quran (reading or recitation) believed to be the final revelation of God. Spoken through the angel Gabriel given to the prophet Muhammad over a period of 23 years. The Quran is actually viewed as an Arabic literary masterpiece. It contains 114

Suras or chapters and 6236 ayat's or verses. Muslims also believe in the Tawrat (Torah) and the Injil (Gospels) but believe them to be too distorted by man to even believe them to be the true Word of God.

4. Muslims have a belief in prophets and their list includes: Adam, Noah, Abraham, Moses and Jesus to name a few. Muhammad is considered to be the seal of all prophets.

5. Resurrection and Judgement: All mankind is to be judged and placed in Jannah (Paradise) or Jahannam (Hell).

6. Divine will: basically consists of the knowledge that everything good or bad is believed to be decreed and nothing can change it. It is the will of Allah.

The five (5) daily prayers (Salat):

1. Fajr or morning prayer consists of two prostrations called Raka's.

2. Zuhr or noon prayer (4 raka's)

3. Asa or afternoon prayer (4 raka's)

4. Maghrib or sunset prayer (3 raka's)

5. Isha or night prayer (4 raka's)

After these prayers are made, Muslims will perform Dua's which are repeated petitions made to God. There are also restrictions dealing with prayer. Prepubescent children and menstruating women and women who have recently given birth within 40 days cannot perform Salat. Muslims also perform a thing called "wudu" which consists of washing certain body parts to be clean before you go into prayer before God. If you at any time relieve yourself, you must completely wash the area and depending on the circumstance you may have to do an "ablution" which is basically a bath/shower. You cannot go before God unclean!

I was bombarded with so much information like the seven Heavens and seven Hells. This was absolutely crazy to me until I looked in the Bible and saw where when Heaven is mentioned it is mentioned in a plural sense in a lot of passages. "The Heaven, even the Heavens, are the Lords" (Genesis 8:2).

That was amazing to me, so I knew that the Quran was surely on to something. If I submitted to God's will, I might have to go to the highest level of Hell for a little while, but it is to cleanse me of the sin that I committed while here on earth. After I am cleansed, I might be able to reach the lowest level of Heaven and live in paradise with virgins and anything I could imagine that Heaven would be. That sounded good to me then but not now. **Think about that for a minute! I was willing to go to Hell temporarily to cleanse my soul!** Who in their right mind would be willing to go to Hell? I was so blinded to the real truth I couldn't have been in my right mind. As I got older, I dug into Islam more and more and there were things that just did not sit well with my spirit. Only during the month of Ramadan, I did feel refreshed or maybe I was too weak to comprehend what I was feeling. Let me tell you – fasting from sunup to sundown for thirty days was no easy task. To this day, if my pastor speaks of a fast (which he doesn't often), I am ready to run and act like I never heard him. Don't let my foolish thoughts or words fool you, we all should fast and pray.

There was so much I had to learn about the religion of Islam that I really didn't believe that I could possibly learn it all. I had to study on the difference in Islam because just like other religions, it has its off shoots and branches that actually form the whole Islamic tree. Let me state that in reality, most Middle Eastern countries do not consider the NOI to be a branch of Islam. I had once asked my friends about it and they said they had never heard of the NOI. I had to get them information so they could read up on this so-called Islam. Once they read the information, they denounced the NOI immediately and asked me how I almost fell for such foolishness. My only reply was that I was mad and hurt. I was looking for a way to get away from the issues that bothered me here in small-town America. That was so embarrassing for me to admit at that time, but it was the truth. The truth remains today. There are plenty of young black and brown brothers who are looking for a spiritual base and find the Nation of Islam very accepting unlike most churches which have a snooty aura about them as soon as you walk in the door. If the church is too judgmental on our youth, why would they want to go to a church like that? But that doesn't just apply to youth coming into a church. A lot of churches have a way of not making you feel welcome. Our pastor emphasizes to us to be very welcoming to visitors and members alike. The first impression will show whether that is a church you would like to attend again in the future. If you go to a church and there are not many members, either their members are disobedient, or they have very bad customer service which means they are not very welcoming.

The person who asked me when I was going to get away from all those Methodists and Baptist was not welcoming. It was degrading and not Christlike to me.

There were terms I had to become familiar with because people would surely ask such questions like what Jihad is. Even unto this day, I hate to hear someone's definition of Jihad who has no knowledge of the faith. It simply means to strive or struggle in the way of Allah against Satan. It does not mean to go out here and start wars against the so-called infidels. For one, Islam does not consider Christians infidels. The Quran actually calls Christians the people of the book. Prophet Muhammad had respect for Christians because of their belief in the Injil (Gospels) and prophets and did not want them persecuted. The only problem with this was that Prophet Muhammad believed Christians had altered the truth of the Gospels. It is mentioned many times in the Holy Quran and is still an argument by faithful Muslims today. They will show you different versions of the Bible and how in their thinking that the message was altered. They will take you to the Council of Nicea 325 AD as proof positive that the gospels we enjoy as our guide today were altered all these years ago. Let me assure you that even some of this is a myth.

We will get into this subject later.

I was a Sunni Muslim and considered the first four (4) Caliphs (leaders) were the right successors to Prophet Muhammad after his death and anyone righteous could eventually become a Caliph. There was also a sect called Shia Muslims who believed the Caliph should be elected by the community and that Prophet Muhammad appointed his successor Ali Talib.

Islam was the world's second largest growing and fastest growing religion in North America. Its holy cities are Mecca, Medina and Jerusalem. The meaning of Islam is simply submission to God/Allah. Submission to God would be no problem for me since I just wanted to do the will of God. I was reading materials at a frantic pace and actually trying to learn Arabic so I could recite Salat properly. Let me say that took years for me. I had to learn from hearing and working with some friends of mine from Saudi Arabia who loved teaching this dumb imbecile how to speak Arabic. They would really get a kick out of it. They would get to the point of challenging me and speak nothing but Arabic. I could decipher some but once they started speaking fast, I was lost. I am not good at learning different languages, just ask my wife. She has worked with me on Spanish for 15 years, but my eight-year-old twins understand and speak it far better than daddy does or will ever be able to.

I believed that Prophet Muhammad was the seal of all the prophets. He was given the The Holy Quran over a period of twenty-three years. Some scholars believe that Muhammad had people around him who informed him about Christianity, and he got some facts distorted. This was to eliminate the possibility that the Quran was divinely inspired. Tradition states that Muhammad was an illiterate man and couldn't have possibly written the text himself. Muslims believe that Jesus predicted Muhammad's coming in the Bible. John 16:7 states "Nevertheless I tell you the truth; It is expedient for you that I go away: for if I go not away, the Comforter will not come unto you; but if I depart I will send him unto you." Muslims believe that the Holy Spirit was already at work in the world and is none other than the angel Gabriel, so it is probable for the Comforter to be none other than the prophet Jesus was speaking of. Muslims adhere to Muhammad's words and ways which is called Sunna; a lot of his sayings are in books called Hadith, but you had to be careful to see which ones were accurate statements from the prophet. A popular version of Hadith in Islam is the Sahih Muslim edition.

There were so many things I was learning in Islam I couldn't possibly grasp all that was given to me. I was living in Richmond, VA and going to The Islamic Center of Virginia which was conveniently right around the corner from my house. I also went to an Islamic Center downtown which used to belong to the Nation of Islam and a lot of those brothers and sisters used to follow Elijah Muhammad but now followed Warith Deen Muhammad and embraced true Islam. I had good times going to the Masjids (the more common word used in the Middle East instead of mosque that is mostly used in North America) in the Richmond area. I even went to the NOI bakeries because they could make some of the best fish sandwiches and bean pies in the world. As in most cities, I could go on the intersection of Belvidere and Broad streets and maybe catch a brother with NOI selling bean pies and The Final Call newspaper so I could see what Minister Farrakhan was talking about. I was totally engrossed in Islamic culture and loved every second of it but there was one problem. I never felt complete. After all these years calling out for Allah and thanking Him for his last messenger prophet Muhammad, I never felt at peace or that my soul was in a good place if I passed away. Let me tell you, if you ever have a doubt about your soul and where it would go if you died right now without any warning, don't fight that feeling. **Get to that altar and get on your knees!** Ask for God's forgiveness and mercy because He will surely guide you alright. I lived like that for years wondering if I would get into Heaven, but once Jesus came into my life, I knew without a shadow of a doubt I am going to Heaven! Don't live life like I did and question everything in your heart. With Jesus your heart will embrace the Holy Spirit, and everything will feel as natural as your own skin. Even when you have HELL going on all around you, when you call out that name JESUS, you will know that He is already at work and is going to do what He promised. I can't truly say that I had that in Islam. I was in Islam for a total of fourteen years (14) and I had always stated that if anybody could show me where Jesus said, "I am God," I would immediately give up Islam and revert back to Christianity. I probably said this with a bit of sarcasm because I just knew nobody could find that exact phrase in the Word because it's not there. How wrong I was! The exact phrase might not have been there, but Jesus said it as plain as day and even after reading the Bible in its entirety to show people how flawed and wrong it was, my whole world was rocked for a moment in time after understanding what a simple phrase really meant.

Back in Southwest Virginia!

I had transferred jobs to the prison in town and at that time nothing had changed as far as my religious beliefs went. I was still acting a fool though, chasing women trying to get my numbers up and heading to every party and club I could get into. Once I hit 30, I realized I need to slow down, get my health in order and for once in my life finally act like a man. I started going to the gym because I had a serious cholesterol problem that came partly from my steady diet of Burger King and my heredity didn't help. My cholesterol was 595 and my triglycerides were well over 1500! My doctor at the time informed me I was a walking stroke and could fall dead at any minute. Not to mention that at times my blood pressure would run high which I attributed to the profession I was in. (I don't know many Correctional Officers who don't have high blood pressure). I also smoked a pack of cigarettes per day so that probably wasn't in my best interest. Let me say that it was harder to quit eating chitlins and pig's feet than it was to stop smoking! (JESUS kept me even in my ignorance. He could have taken me out, but He chose to keep me here because I had a purpose that He was going to use me for! Thank you JESUS!) Again, I was not sure about my soul because my practice of Islam was not feeling natural at this time. So instead of looking for Jesus, let's just get my cholesterol right which I did with an aggressive diet and medication regimen. I got my total cholesterol level to 69. Still working on triglycerides, but overall, my bloodwork is now good. Thank you Lord!

I started going back to college to finally get my degree in Criminal Justice. Bluefield is a private religious school so of course I had to take a religious class to graduate. I figured I would get in this class and refute any doctrine he exposed me to and show how the Bible in fact was not the Word of God. He started the class saying that for centuries people have been trying to dispute the Word of the Bible and prove that it was inaccurate. He didn't know that I was one of those people. He did say one thing that would make me give him a break. He stated that although people have shown some inaccuracies, the Bible had so many prophecies that had come true he would stick with the Bible as his source to God. I could not dispute that. There were plenty of things happening in the world that would prove the Bible true in its current form no matter which version you preferred. One night he was discussing the Deity and he stated that a lot of people, even those who believed in the trinity, believed that Jesus Christ was God. I started to get antsy and I wanted to show this professor of Theology who took divinity classes at Duke University how wrong he was and show him all the education in the world could not prove Jesus was nothing more than a prophet. He explained that the phrase "I am" actually meant in Hebrew I am God. I had heard the phrase about the great I am but never knew what it meant. I just figured it was a name God called himself in the Old Testament. This is when he blew my socks off! It might not have as much meaning to you, but this verse literally saved my soul. In John 8: 58 –

58 Jesus said unto them, Verily, verily, I say unto you, Before Abraham was, I am.

I tell folks that sometimes when I try to explain what made me return to Christianity, but they don't understand what that verse meant to me and maybe never will. When he showed the class that verse, that professor will never know what he did to me that night. You could have bought me for a penny! He had single handedly shown me something that would ever change the course of how I lived my life from that moment on. I went home that night and contemplated that verse over and over again until there was no other choice but to get on my hands and knees and pray for forgiveness. You can see there are so many instances where Jesus is spoken of in the Old Testament and the prophet Isaiah speaks of Jesus many times.

Isaiah 7:14

14 Therefore the Lord himself shall give you a sign; Behold, a virgin shall conceive, and bear a son, and shall call his name Immanuel.

Isaiah 40:3-5

3 The voice of him that crieth in the wilderness, Prepare ye the way of the LORD, make straight in the desert a highway for our God.

4 Every valley shall be exalted, and every mountain and hill shall be made low: and the crooked shall be made straight, and the rough places plain:

5 And the glory of the LORD shall be revealed, and all flesh shall see *it* together: for the mouth of the LORD hath spoken *it*.

Here the prophet obviously speaks of John the Baptist

preparing people for the coming of the living God.

Isaiah 53: 5

5 But he *was* wounded for our transgressions, *he was* bruised for our iniquities: the chastisement of our peace *was* upon him; and with his stripes we are healed.

You have to forgive my excitement as I reflect now, I know of no other who can heal like The Great I Am, Jesus Christ! I thanked the Lord for showing me Him because I had lost my life in that spiritual state… I told Jesus that night I was getting away from all the foolishness that I had been participating in and was going to live my life for Him. The song "Second Chance" from a Hezekiah Walker CD to this day tears me up because that is exactly what Jesus had just given me. I had officially become a Jesus freak!

Jesus or the Devil?

There came a time in my life where I was just always confused. Mentally and spiritually, I just didn't feel like I could get myself together. I did know that Jesus was the center of my life but there was a period that I wondered about why I started going through turmoil after rededicating my life to Jesus. I had a girlfriend who had just broken off our engagement, I was not happy at work, my finances were not exactly where I wanted them to be and basically I wanted things to change for the good. I was barely eating and still smoking like a freight train. I spent a lot of my free time playing ball or at the gym just to burn off steam. I still didn't have a church home and was very skeptical about some of the churches in town because of the members. I thought devoting my life to Jesus, everything would turn around, but I found out that once you take that first step toward Jesus, the devil is going to come at you like a roaring lion. The devil kept me from joining a church because I thought most of the people in the churches I knew of were hypocrites and I didn't want to be bothered with that foolishness. One night I was hanging out with my friend and distant cousin who later would become my Pastor, Bishop Robert Nolan Wolfe. He would sing karaoke at a spot in Bristol, Virginia, and I went with him that night, but I felt like a fish out of water. He knew I was in a funk about a failed relationship and about life in general. He also knew there was one thing that could help me get back on track. Her name was Denise Morales!

My bishop and I were sitting out in the parking lot watching people and he leaned over to me and said, "Bumpy (one of my many nicknames), you need to call Denise." Anybody who knows me knew I had loved Denise for a long time. She was my best friend and we stayed in contact with each other even when we were miles apart. I loved her but never had the courage to tell her until she had moved back to New York and was miles away from me. She had left New York and had settled in Galax, Virginia, so we were just an hour away now. I looked over and I said, "Mudd (short for Muddfoot, his nickname), you must be crazy! She was in Galax now, but she is doing her own thing. Buckwhite (Childhood friend Keith Combs) told me the same thing a day or so ago. Y'all gotta be crazy! Mudd was like just give her a call and see what's up." I called her the next night, it was nothing unusual just the same crap talking I always did with her, but I was kind of seeing if she was with someone or not. Let me just say we had approximately two dates and I have been married to my best friend ever since. My point is Jesus was there the whole time while I was in my funk and depressed! I was trying to keep something together that God meant to tear apart. When you are going through, you don't realize God is setting these things before you to bring you closer to Him. Had I married the previous young lady I was engaged to, God only knows what might have happened because it was not in God's will for us to be together. You never want to be or do anything outside of God's will. He will close the door on you and set obstacles in your way to keep you from doing things that are outside of His will. In turn, you have to constantly pray and discern what He wants for your life. From July 26, 2006, my wife and I have agreed to try our best to stay in God's will. That's the only way things can stay together is if it is ordained by God.

Sometimes it feels that as you go in life, the devil will try and throw all kinds of things at you just to see if you will fall away from God. I have felt that pressure before and the beginning of November 2008. While growing up my father, Floyd Benjamin Stanback, was never around. He did his thing in Washington D.C and we were in a rural part of Virginia and he never once called to check on me. That is the number one reason that I never changed my name back to Stanback once I renounced Islam. That man didn't deserve for me to carry his last name and I hate it when someone calls me by Stanback. For one thing, it shows that you either don't know me or never respected my decision for the name change because if you really knew how I felt about that name and still say it, you should say it in fear. I have literally had to restrain myself from using language I don't use anymore when someone will call me Stanback. I have always told my wife that anyone who calls me by that name isn't a friend of mine anyway. The absence of my real father was fine with me because I had an uncle, Captain Gregory Beale Steele, Jr., (aka Bubba). He was part of the US Army. He who was an uncle, father, brother and friend all wrapped up in one. I would visit him as much as possible when I was younger because I thought he was the coolest man ever. If I was ever in need, there was never a doubt that he would get me what I needed or wanted. If I needed to have a boot put on my backside, he could do it over the phone. He was really a big teddy bear but if you got on his bad side, just stay away from the stare. He was a fairly large man, 6'4 in height and his weight could fluctuate like everybody else in our family so we won't even bring that up. He was sort of a local legend around here because of his athletic ability. There just wasn't a sport he wasn't good at, but everyone knew him for wrestling in high school. Never won states but never placed lower than third. If you have ever wrestled, you know that is quite an accomplishment. I always wanted to be like him, but I didn't inherit his genes in that matter. He used to tell me I was just lazy. He would be blunt but that's what I loved about Bubba. We would talk almost every day especially after he retired from the military. We would talk about absolutely nothing or he would complain to me about his sister and my mother, but he never failed to call her every day and any time of day. There is a ten-year difference in the age, and I believe my mom thought of him as more of a son than a brother. When she first moved to DC, she would bring him up there or if he needed something, he would ask her first before he would ask my grandmother. They were close and he was actually thinking about bringing her to live with him but that couldn't happen until he slowed down a little bit with work if that was at all possible. He was a workaholic to say the least and I actually believed he loved work. I remember I was sitting at home one Sunday after church and I was thinking I had talked to Bubba Friday, but I didn't have time to fool with him, so the call was short. That week before, he had blown up my phone and it was a busy week for me at work, so it took a while to see what he wanted and when I talked to him Friday, he was just checking on me. I figured I would give him a call after the game and see what he was doing later. I saw a call coming from my mom and when I answered all I could hear was her sobbing hysterically. I never did figure out what was going on. All I could decipher was someone had died. I handed the phone to my wife to try and figure it out because I could not understand what my mom was saying. I thought maybe her older brother, Hurley Steele (Billy), had passed unexpectedly or something. Don't believe I am making light of that because I love my uncle Billy too. In my narrow mind, I always figured if anybody went first that it would be my mom because her health wasn't the best but since Billy was older. I could see him going first. I was not ready when my wife finally told me that my uncle Bubba had passed away. She told me he was at home and had been on the phone with work and after he hung up, he just slumped over and fell on the floor. I felt like I had been shot in the gut. I was trying to be strong and deal with it like I would expect him to deal with death, but my eyes were not cooperating. My safety net was gone, and I really had a feeling of being alone. I had to go to Marion and check on my mom and get some plane tickets so I could make sure she would be in Fort Worth, Texas as soon as possible. She went down the next day and my wife and I went down a couple of days later. As I said, my eyes were not cooperating with me at all. All of the "I wish I had done this before they died" stuff was in my head and there were so many things I wish I could have said to him, but I figured I had 30 years or more before I would have to worry about it. Let me just say that we never know God's plan, so we better tell the folks we love how we feel about them every day because you just never know. I still struggle with that even after my uncle's incident because I don't talk to his wife, my favorite aunt Karen, like I should. It is just hard for me to speak with her or his kids Gregory and Jeremy. They just remind me so much of him, especially Jeremy because since the day he was born he has looked like Bubba literally spit him out. The older he gets, the more he looks like him. Only when Jeremy has long hair can I tell the difference between the two. I think Gregory looks like me a little bit when I have my glasses on. He and Jeremy are quite a bit taller than me and not as big, but people thought my uncle and I favored so maybe it's a Steele thing. Once we got to Texas, it was just one regret after another. I remember after Denise and I got married, he called me later that night. I thought it was going to be congratulations on the marriage but instead it was the first time I remember my uncle actually being mad at me because he called me an asshole. He had never spoken to me like that before, so I was shocked to say the least. He was mad because I never told him the date of the wedding and he missed it. I tried to tell him that I just never gave a date because I knew our wedding was going to be about ten minutes, nothing big and lavish so I didn't want him to come to Virginia all the way from Texas for something that wasn't lavish. He really got heated then because he told me he didn't care, and he wanted to be there, and I believe his feelings were truly hurt. I have regretted that I didn't have my uncle at my wedding because he was surely my best man and he could have calmed my nerves before the wedding waiting on my wife because she was 30 minutes late. Knowing him, he probably would have made fun of me because he was always the jokester. I remember when I finally got to put eyes on my uncle I just lost it. My body finally caught up with my eyes and was in mourning. I remember my aunt standing beside me telling me to just talk with him, but I was mad at him for leaving me alone with no one to really confide in about things. We had made plans on how to deal with my mother as she got older. There were just so many things reeling in my head that I had to actually run out of that funeral home. I spoke with God a lot on that trip because I didn't understand how if He knew my uncle was so vital to me, why would He take him at such a young age at that time. I had many more questions for God, but I kept in the back of my mind, His will be done. That helped soothe some of the pain but even today, I just want to pick up the phone and hear that voice, that laugh, that instruction and words of wisdom. I would love to hear my uncle one more time so I could tell him all the things I want. I will get that chance again when we meet in Heaven but until then I love and miss you, Bubba!

There was another time that I really questioned why God let the devil mess with me. One day after church service, I was lying around the house watching my beloved Lakers and my wife walks by me and says that she feels nauseated. Half-jokingly, I told her maybe she was pregnant. We had been working on that for over a year with no success, so I really didn't think anything of the statement. When she returned from the bathroom she said that the test she just took confirmed what I had said. MY WIFE IS PREGNANT! She could not have given me better news than that on that particular day. My mind was racing! I'm calling everybody I can because we are going to have a kid. We would proceed as usual for the time being. I bought books to see what we would need to be prepared so I could get acclimated for fatherhood. I checked with our landlord and let her know we are going to need a bigger apartment because the one-bedroom place we had was not going to cut it. She was excited as we were and made sure that if any two or three-bedroom apartments opened up, it was ours. We called the doctor and made an appointment for her to be seen on the following Wednesday. Everything was looking good except the fact that my wife didn't have morning sickness. Instead, she was sick all the time. We finally went to the doctor and he told us he could hear a heartbeat, and everything looked good. He said sickness would be part of the process and it was nothing to worry about. The next day when my wife was at work, she returned home early, and I asked her what was wrong. She looked pale and she said she just didn't feel good.

We got another appointment and when we return to the doctor, he informs us that she has to go on immediate bed rest. We are just a couple of months into this pregnancy and she is already on bedrest. I babied her as much as possible, but she just never felt well. She would try to eat but she would never keep anything down. I remember one night, I was actually laughing at this later, but this particular night she wanted some hot wings, and I ran to the store to get them. She ate those things as fast as my wife has ever eaten hoping to hold it down. The baby wasn't having it! She might have kept those wings down for ten minutes if that. This lasted for about three months and I felt helpless because I knew my love was miserable but what could I do? I stayed in prayer for things to improve and for her to deliver a healthy baby. The sex didn't matter, I just wanted a healthy baby. I knew Jesus would fix it because He said, "Ask and you shall receive." One day while watching TV, she screamed for me to come into the bathroom. My wife is a very private person so a call like this does not happen. When I get there, she is sitting on the toilet like she is about to pass out. I ran and got her a glass of water so the dizziness would go away. She was crying and once I helped her up, I saw she was hemorrhaging so much. I pride myself on staying calm when there is a type of emergency going on. I would not let my wife know but I was freaking out. I work in a prison and have seen things that could make the devil flinch, but I have never seen so much blood in my life. It was literally running down her leg and I had no idea what to do. After a couple more bathroom trips, we managed to get her dressed and we headed to the doctor's office which was an hour away. It felt like I got there in 20 minutes. I was flying! I had called the doctor when we were on the way and once we got there, they took her straight back to the office and got her set up for examination. I can't even get close to her because so many nurses and doctors are in the small little office trying to figure out what's going on. I watch the doctor and I see a puzzled look come over his face and here comes my anxiety. I stay strong for my wife because I don't want her to think I'm worried, but my stomach is doing flips. I did not like the look her doctor had on his face and he brought in his wife who is also a doctor to assess the situation. Both of them looked like they had just forgotten everything they were taught while they were looking at that sonogram. The doctor informed the nurses to get an ambulance and get my wife admitted to the hospital, give her some pain meds and he would be over. I tried to look at the sonogram, but I never could get close enough to see what was going on. I kissed Denise on the head and told her I was going to be right behind her and everything was going to be alright. As I got in the car, I lost it. I didn't have my usual man of reason to help give me advice. Bubba had just passed away that previous November. I am sitting in the car losing my mind staring at my phone thinking, who am I going to call? It was at that moment I realized it was time for me to grow up and find my own answers. My crutch was gone when I needed him the most, but he had prepared me for how to deal with certain situations and I was going to be put to the test now. I got to the hospital and I know the doctor beat me there. Denise had stopped bleeding and he just wanted her to rest overnight and we would assess the situation the next morning. Once she fell asleep, I went back to Wytheville to get us both a change of clothes and just let my mind wander for a little bit. I have recently heard my pastor speak of trying to pray but there are just no words. I couldn't talk because it felt like someone had gut-checked me and I was having a hard time breathing. It felt like there was an elephant on my chest and I didn't have time to be having a heart attack now. I had a feeling of grief, but Denise and the baby were fine so why couldn't I talk to God? On the ride back to the hospital, I called my mother and Denise's brother,

Victor, and let them know what was going on. I don't know where it came from because I didn't even want to entertain the thought of it, but I distinctly remember telling Victor that Denise is going to lose the baby. I said that out of nowhere and when I finally realized what I had said, I was literally getting cussed out by her brother for even thinking about it. I got back to the hospital and Denise was resting so I just laid back and began to beg God that everything would be alright but something in my spirit said otherwise. She slept fairly comfortably for most of the night without much pain going on with her. That morning, the usual slew of nurses came by and checked on her and I began to become less nervous because whatever happened with Denise and her body was over. I figured that the doctor would come in and check her out and we head to the house. Finally, a nurse showed up and she said the doctor wanted to see Denise in some other part of the hospital. We got down there and wherever we were just felt cold and damp to me. They moved Denise to the bed with stirrups in it and he started examining her. As quickly as he bent down to look, I heard him say, "Damn!" I could tell by the way he said it that it wasn't good. He turned around and got the forceps and he pulled our baby boy out. I went over to Denise to console her, but I was really in shock.

He began to tell us that for the most part the baby was healthy, but it did not have room to grow in the womb. Denise had fibroid tumors and an old wife's tale said that if you got pregnant, the tumors would shrink. Let me tell you that is a lie straight from the pits of Hell. Her tumors grew so big you could see on the sonograms that he would be in a tight space. The doctor had been talking and I really don't remember what he said later on, but I do remember they left us there in the room by ourselves and besides holding each other, what more was there to say? After a while, we went back to the room and I couldn't pull my head up to really look at Denise, but I had to be strong and hopefully say the right things to give her ease at the time. Finally, a nurse came back to the room with the baby cleaned up with a little cute skull cap on his head. We each held him and showed each other parts of Junior that looked like each other. I know for sure he had those Morales/Gloria hands and feet, big with the nail area flat as a board. The doctor finally came into the room and we could tell he had been in tears, but he got himself together and told us our options for the body. The doctor told us that when Denise showed up at his office the day before, the reason he kept looking at the sonogram was because he didn't see the baby or any fluid in her womb.

Basically, she was in a type of labor but way too premature. He was hoping for the best but he knew what he was going to be looking at when he had her brought down that morning. He asked whether we wanted a memorial or just wanted to leave the body there at the hospital. Leaving the body was not an option! We continued talking and he left us with Junior so we could have time with him. At that particular time, I have to admit that might have been the darkest time in my life. Bubba had just died a couple of months earlier and now my child never even got a chance to take a good breath and he was gone. I have told only a few people this, but I have never been so mad and disgusted with God in all my life. It was never a fact of me not believing in Him, but I wanted to know why. Why did you do this to us? We are trying to live a life for Christ, and He does this to us! You take my uncle and now my boy. During that time, if He had taken me, I could not have cared less. I was in some pain and really had no one to even talk to about it. I was a man. I was just going to buck up and deal with it! I didn't have the revelation or discernment that during times like these you PRAISE HIM ANYWAY! You have to learn to praise Him even when you just want to mourn. You PRAISE HIM ANYWAY! I will be the first to tell you, it's easier said than done but you have to let the Holy Ghost guide you.

We had my son, Gregory Alexander Abdullah Rashad, Jr., cremated. When we finally took his ashes home, everything started to feel okay, but I still had questions as to why God, knowing that if we tried to have another child the same thing would happen, why would He take the one thing I really wanted? MY BOY. I know it rocked Denise because I remember going to church before the memorial service and the pastor asked her if he could pray for her and I remember her saying no. She was so hurt, and I am guessing just felt at the time that prayer obviously would not work. That was one thing during that whole time I have never asked her about, nor do I have any intention of asking why she refused prayer. We had been praying the whole time but to no avail, Junior was gone. We finally got back in a routine again after a couple of weeks. We got in a workflow and we were still going to church every Sunday, but it started to become a chore. I was still pissed, and I felt we were just going because that's what we were supposed to do. Any activities held at church besides Sunday service we would shy away from. We became more involved in our Masonic and Eastern Star lodges and went to work. That was what we did for a little while to help ease the pain of our loss. Our Pastor at the time, Dr. Weldon, who we loved retired not long after all of this happened due to health problems and we got a new pastor at that particular Methodist church we were attending in Wytheville, VA. I hate to admit this but it's true. When she arrived at the church, that church became the most boring congregation I had ever seen in my life. She had no fire or spirit and really I can't remember one sermon that she spoke the whole time we were there. We dealt with that for a couple of years. Some Sundays, I would just look over at Denise and ask if she wanted to go to church and of course the response would be no. Only if Dr. Weldon came back or his wife, Pastor Weldon, would we make haste to get to church. I could not hear our other pastor tell me how much God loved us. How many ways can you put that into a sermon until it becomes monotonous? Basically, she was giving her congregation the spiritual milk that I had heard for years and I was yearning for that spiritual meat. Those words that make you reflect on life and cringe. My anger had dissipated with God and I understood He had a plan, and I will never know what it is. I can guess what it was, but we will discuss this later. As for that spiritual meat I was yearning for, all I can say is the Lord got jokes too. Luckily for us because of a government takeover and something called rural development, they kicked us out of our apartment for making too much money. (I'm not a Republican but I understand! I can't win for losing here). They moved us out of our apartment so I guess a person could come in and pay $50 a month rent instead of the $600 we were paying. Let me say that God has a funny way of getting me to move but I believe His plan worked.

Antioch Greater Love Ministries

God has jokes! We came back to Marion and decided to stay at the house that I grew up in. My mom was having a hard time keeping up the house and I had to spend almost as much time there as I did at my house because of the stuff she would need with groceries and cleaning around the house. There was only so much cleaning that could be done because my mom was a classic pack rat! She fit the definition of a hoarder in every sense of the word but will deny it to this day. I knew my wife would have a serious problem living like that and I had been away from the house for years so that would be an adjustment for me as well. We put most of our stuff in storage and we cleaned what we could at my mother's house. We stayed in the room a lot and worked as much as possible just to get out of the house. We were still going to the Methodist church in Wytheville, but I figured surely there were churches going in Marion that we could attend. We just had to find one where we felt comfortable and received good Word. I couldn't think of one place that I wanted to go besides maybe Mudd's (Bishop Wolfe) church, but my wife was adamant she was not going to that church. I said okay. I have some reservations about some of the people who went there because some kept the gossip mill running and I didn't want to be a part of that. We decided to go to Wytheville at least one more time for Easter service. I remember we took some friends of ours who were looking for a church to attend also. I don't mean to be rude, that was the wrong time to take them. The service was so boring! I was actually falling asleep during service and it was drawn out, so it felt like torture. When we all got back in the car and went out to eat, I told everybody that was the last straw. I could not take any more of the long drawn-out and monotonous sermons she was delivering. I had asked people about how they felt about the Pastor and they would say they just pull out a book and read it or browse on their smartphones, but they were not leaving the church they grew up in. To me, that appeared risky because that is something that could deliver your soul to Hell. If you are not receiving good Word, why would you stay in a church just because you grew up in it? My wife and I made a decision that we would find a church in Marion and just stay in the background until we find one we like. I was talking to Mudd and he said to come on down to his church, their service didn't start until 6:00 pm. Man, he just made my day because I get up early every day for work and I want just one of my off days to sleep in. This was going to be perfect! My wife and I spoke about going to Mudd's all week but she really wasn't interested about becoming a member and was adamant about the fact at times. We finally went to the church that Sunday and man, I knew Mudd knew the Word but good Lord! He knocked it out of the park that day! There weren't many people there and I had come to find out that a lot of people left and went elsewhere. I have also come to find out that there are a couple of good reasons why church attendance and church rolls will not be as full as they should. They never invested in kids, the pastor continues to feed the flock milk, or the pastor comes straight from the Bible and exposes the members which shows that people will run from GOOD WORD. God's Word is hard to handle sometimes but I beg you not to get mad at the pastor, get mad at what you see in the mirror. The visit to the church instantly changed my wife's mind. I remember her saying on the ride back home that she learned more in that hour and a half than she has ever learned in all of these years of going to church. It wasn't long before we sent a letter to our former church and informed them of our move of membership to another church. Now Antioch Greater Love Ministries is an apostolic church which believes in the oneness of God i.e., Jesus is God; He wrapped himself in flesh and came to earth to redeem the whole of humanity. They also believe in water baptism in Jesus' name and the infilling of the Holy Ghost. 1 "And when the day of Pentecost was fully come, they were all with one accord in one place (Acts 2; 1-4).

2 And suddenly there came a sound from heaven as of a rushing mighty wind, and it filled all the house where they were sitting.

3 And there appeared unto them cloven tongues like as of fire, and it sat upon each of them.

4 And they were all filled with the Holy Ghost, and began to speak with other tongues, as the Spirit gave them utterance."

Also look at Acts 2; 36-39 with emphasis on verse 38.

36 "Therefore let all the house of Israel know assuredly, that God hath made that same Jesus, whom ye have crucified, both Lord and Christ.

37 Now when they heard *this*, they were pricked in their heart, and said unto Peter and to the rest of the apostles, Men *and* brethren, what shall we do?

38 Then Peter said unto them, Repent, and be baptized every one of you in the name of Jesus Christ for the remission of sins, and ye shall receive the gift of the Holy Ghost.

39 For the promise is unto you, and to your children, and to all that are afar off, *even* as many as the Lord our God shall call."

A lot of our faith is based upon these passages of scripture. For years there have been debates on the formula of baptism and after reading Acts 2; 38, how can there be any debate? God's Word is right there in front of us and we are so hardheaded, we are still having doubts and debates.

Twin Terrorists!

I remember one Sunday we were sitting in church and my friend and elder, Prophetess Tammi Turner, walked to the back where my wife and I were sitting. She told Denise that something in her spirit told her to do it. She placed her hands on Denise's stomach and began to pray hard in the spirit. I had no clue what was going on, but I continued singing during praise and worship service. I later found out that Tammi had informed her she was getting her womb ready for children. I knew I had informed Tammi that Denise had a hysterectomy years ago. When we got home, I said that's cool if it would work but that's not how it works in the real world. It shows just how spiritually ignorant I was at that time. We never knew that the prophetess was preparing my wife for a spiritual birth. As time went on we spoke of it but in our carnal minds, we could not see the pieces falling into place for one of the greatest moments of our lives. I believe it was a year or so later that my cousin Samantha calls me and says she needs to talk to me. She asked if we could meet somewhere out in town to discuss something. Anything for my cousin, but I became apprehensive when people want to meet in person instead of speaking on the phone. If it's that important, then it usually is not good. We met at McDonald's in Marion and she began to tell me about her friend who was a young lady who had four kids already and was pregnant with twin boys. Samantha wanted to know if Denise and I wanted to adopt the boys. I think my jaw hit the floor! I was ecstatic and could not wait to go home and tell Denise. Denise was overjoyed but we knew that there would have to be some drastic changes around our house. We had basically opened ourselves up for Social Services to pry around in our house and finances. We knew it would be worth the intrusion, but you still dread people coming to your house to inspect anything. Operation cleanup was underway to clear away the junk that my mother thought was important for some reason. Let me let you in on a hoarder's mindset for just a moment. There was a Jet magazine from 1973 that my mother told us not to throw away because she had not read it! A toy that was given to me from my grandmother sometime in the 70's I decided I was going to throw away. My mother started crying over that toy truck because to her

I was getting rid of memories. To a hoarder, memories are things, not the memories in your heart. My uncle Billy tries to explain that when they were younger, they never threw anything away. I understand those were different times, but I think my mother went to another level that was dangerous to her health and well-being. This gives them a reason to keep everything because everything has a memory. I was determined that I would not let my kids live like that because for one, it is embarrassing, and it is just not healthy. To this day, my mother thinks we throw things away behind her back but most likely it is stored away in a tote to be thrown away at a later date. She is in a nursing home now so I know the totes will be discarded. I like order wherever I am, whether it is my desk in the office, home or car, everything has a place. Anyway, we haul off junk for days and finally have the house in order. We retain the services of a lawyer to whom we are forever grateful because she took our calls on weekends when we thought there may be issues. Her paralegal was always in court to help and assist us through the process. We had spoken to the young lady and she agreed to the adoption and signed her rights away to the boys knowing that at any time she could be active in their lives. Let me just say that I understand why people go overseas to adopt children. The United States has put so much red tape in the process that it has turned me off from ever wanting to adopt any more kids. It was one legal thing after another, and it eventually took us almost two years to have the adoption finalized. What a pain in the behind but I must say it was all worth it!

I will never forget that day, January 12, 2013. We were getting ready to go to my sister- in-law's house when the young lady called around 10:00 am that Saturday morning and said she was getting ready to go to the hospital because the doctors were going to go ahead and deliver the boys. I was cool until that call and then it was like my stomach stayed in knots until I put my eyes on them. I remember Denise and I went to the store to get last minute items we thought we might need for the boys. I do remember the young lady had told us that she had to drop her other kids off with her mother and would be at the hospital after that. I remember we got to the hospital and the young lady had not gotten there yet. Once I saw her walk in, it was game on. I was trying to act cool about the whole situation but in my heart, I was bursting with praise for my Lord and Savior. I know I will never begin to understand what God does, but in

His infinite wisdom He knew when we were suffering with the loss of Junior that He would bless us doubly. We just have to be patient and lean on His wisdom and understanding and not our own. We had to call our attorney because the babies were born in Tennessee and adoption laws were a little bit different than in Virginia. One of the nurses didn't want to give custody over to us because of the difference in state law. This sent my wife into forms of panic and then rage. I don't like seeing either so I knew our lawyer would get everything straight which she did. They came later and told us they would get us a room but just in case they need the room for a patient, we would have to leave. I am not good with times but if I remember correctly it was around 3:25 pm that a nurse came around the corner with two little bundles of joy each weighing in at around five pounds and one ounce. There were tears of joy as we held them for the first time and then fear gripped me again because I knew that these boys were under our care and I would be responsible for how they grew up in this cruel world. One of the boys was kind of long and lean looking and cranky as hell! The other one was just as calm with fat cheeks and knees pulled up to his chest. At that moment, I knew their nicknames would be Slim and Chunky. Jeremiah Trayvon Gregory Rashad aka Tray aka

Slim was the oldest by a minute. Nehemiah Tyrese Miguel Rashad aka Ty aka Chunky was a mama's boy from day one. We couldn't get enough of them, but the young lady wanted to spend time with them first and then we would get them. We understood that had to be one of the hardest things to ever do so we gave her time with the kids. It was time for us to go and get something to eat. I could hardly eat for being nervous and I just wanted to give God praise for what He had done. We were blessed with two beautiful, healthy baby boys and I can only speak for myself, but I had not really done anything to deserve such a blessing. I was so mad at God when we lost Junior that there wasn't praise in my mouth. I eventually accepted the reality that He is God, and He handles His business as He sees fit and I should praise Him anyway whether – good or bad!

The young lady called and said she was going to bed and she would talk to us tomorrow, so we drove back to the hospital and just loved the boys. We couldn't get enough of them but when it was time to get some sleep. Tray did not want to cooperate with either one of us. If you weren't holding him, he would start crying. If you picked him up, he was quiet as a mouse. This drove me crazy because I could not figure out what would soothe him. The nurse came and got him and Ty later on so we could get some rest. I should have peaked to see what the nurse's secret was because I remember checking on him during the night and they were sound asleep, and the nurses were eating lunch and playing cards. It was nothing but praise for me that whole weekend we were in the hospital with the kids because God had just blessed our souls with these two babies. I hate to think what might have happened to the boys had we not decided to adopt them. Would we have adopted them if Junior was still here? That is a question that bothers me even today because I have such a love for these boys I shudder at the thought of them being passed around from family member to family member and not being around someone to call Mom or Dad. It just shows me that God has a plan for these boys' lives, and I pray I am able to see what He has in store for them in the future. I am also afraid for them because sometimes when God uses you, you have to go through some things to press out some oil for later use. If you don't know what that means, then you haven't let God use you to your fullest spiritual ability. Don't think that I am criticizing you because I need to make sure I have enough oil saved up for my family and me for use at a later date. Ask your pastor about that spiritual oil. It will give you praise like never before and it might save your life. Just like an olive, it has to be pressed to get the oil out. God uses us in the same fashion. We go through trials and tribulations so we can endure for Christ.

"And not only so, but we glory in tribulations also: knowing that tribulation worketh patience" (Romans 5:3 KJV).

"Rejoicing in hope, patient in tribulation: continuing instant in prayer" (Romans 12:12 KJV).

The first night we were able to take the kids to church there was just a feeling I had the whole time, and I could not figure it out. We were there and we checked on Tray who had been sleeping in his carrier, but he looked pale. We shook him and did everything in our power to awaken him, but he was unresponsive. The first thing I could think of was that his sugar was low. He had a problem from birth where his sugar would run between 70-80. He would get a little cranky but after he ate, it would be okay. That night, we just could not rouse him awake to get him to eat. Our pastor and the members went into hard prayer. We left church and went straight to the ER. He became a little alert once we got to the hospital and they started giving him his milk. Once he became fully alert, he finished the bottle. That was unusual for him, but he got his sugar tested and it was in the high 80's. We continued to let him drink on another bottle and we went back to church. When church was about to end, the Bishop stopped everything and said the Lord had told him if I started to praise Him right now, I would receive the Holy Ghost which is speaking in other/foreign tongues. I bet I didn't get one hallelujah out when it became very hard for me to even get anything else out. God's spirit came upon me and I assure you it knocked me on my butt literally! What a feeling to receive the Holy Ghost! To know for sure Jesus' spirit is inside you. I was so happy and relieved to finally have it. It just assured me that Jesus was who I needed to follow all along. I watched the video and when all was said and done, I was lying up under a piano and Bishop did his dance. As he does with everybody, he asked me what I got that night and of course I said I got the Holy Ghost. It was an unreal experience – the power of God was in that house that night. Bishop did warn me after all the euphoria and excitement of the moment, he told me beware because the devil is mad now and he will throw all kinds of things at me to get me back away from God. I believe that night the devil tried to use my kids as a weakness at the time to keep me from church and from receiving the Holy Ghost. My pastor did not lie. All kinds of things were thrown at me but when you have the Holy Ghost, you can feel when something is not right. Your spirit will tell you that you need to dig deeper in prayer. You need to get the prayer warriors praying and warring with and for you. Praise like you have never praised before! I am not saying that the trial will be lifted from you, but you will have been prayed up to where you are better able to handle the situation because you know God would not take you there unless He had a plan for you to come out and give praise and testimony like never before. Remember that spiritual oil I was speaking of earlier? These are the times you use it. In the end, every tribulation we may go through ends up being for God's glory. If I have to go through these things in life which the Bible tells us will happen, I would rather go through it with God guiding and directing me than without.

Covid–19

My pastor had been prophesying and said there would be a time of accelerated death. He started seeing these visions, dreams and letting us know about them in 2016. Sure enough, there were celebrities, pastors and friends of ours that suddenly passed, and we were going to their funerals. Kind of weird, but I had to learn to listen to prophetic voices. You can tell prophetic voices by their fruit. I don't accept everyone with a prophetic voice. I have heard plenty of people speak a prophecy and it never came to fruition. I wait to see if what they say comes true. Our pastor has that voice and the stuff he has told us has come true, whether good or bad. Check their fruit!

Well, one night at watch service on December 31, 2019 as we were bringing the New Year in and everybody was praising God and celebrating, our pastor stopped and told us not to get too excited about the upcoming year because this will be a hard one. God was taking back His church and anybody who stood in the way of that would see their demise. We needed to pray for pastors because the accelerated death was still upon us. We needed to get prayed up and prepare for 2020! I now introduce you to Covid-19. A virus that originated in Wuhan, China and made its way to the United States in early January 2020. It changed our entire way of life. I learned terms like social distancing, and we had to wear masks to try and prevent the spread of the disease. People were getting it and dying, young, old, it didn't matter. They shut down schools and as I type this in January of 2021, my children are still in virtual learning. The churches stopped congregating, restaurants and businesses closed, and vacations were cancelled. We started having church outside and Bible class on this app called Zoom. Our entire way of life was turned upside down. The message almost every week was to prepare for the Lord because we just didn't know what tomorrow would bring. When it hit home for me is in May, early June. We went back into the church for Pentecost Sunday. What a service we had! God moved in the church that day. We really couldn't socially distance that day, but we wore our masks. That Tuesday, our pastor informed us that someone had come to our church that had Covid. That sent my wife into instant panic, but we figured we wore our masks, and we would be alright. A couple of days later, our pastor informed us that he and his wife had Covid and there were a couple of people in the congregation that had come down with the virus. Next thing I know, the person who sat next to my wife put on Facebook that she had contracted the virus. My wife scheduled a Covid test just to make sure she didn't have it. While I was at the doctor's office scheduling a gallbladder surgery a couple of days later, my wife called me inside and said that she was positive. She was going to call our pediatrician to get the boys checked out. I thank God every day that she was asymptomatic. Since the kids had been with us, the doctor assumed the boys had it because they had mild symptoms but no breathing issues. We just had to keep an eye on them to make sure their symptoms didn't get worse. I figured if they got it, I probably had it, but hopefully I would be asymptomatic like my wife. I wound up waiting just a couple of days before I went to get tested. I had developed some symptoms and went to get checked. After that test, I really started to get sick. On June 23, I got the worst news I wanted to hear. My childhood friend, more like family, Prophetess Tammi Turner, passed away from Covid. That hurt me to my soul because she was one of my first childhood girlfriends, but we had always stayed close. She babysat for our kids when we needed her. She was always there when my wife would turn to her about spiritual matters or just shooting the breeze. She was such a loss and I mourned so hard for her, but I had enough sense to know that God knows best, and He took her to be with Him. I had a rough day, and my wife was keeping check on me and taking care of me like she always does. She asked me before I went to sleep if I wanted to go to the hospital and I remember telling her that I wasn't going to no doggone hospital. Well, sometime during the night, my O2 level dropped to 69. I was unaware that I wasn't breathing properly. I remember telling my wife that it was alright and to just let me get some rest. Next thing I know, my wife has someone from the doctor's office on the phone and they are telling me I needed to go to the emergency room. This is the first time in my life that I have ever been mad at my wife. We literally don't argue! I was so mad at her. I didn't want to speak to her. It took me two hours to get out of bed, take a shower and put clothes on to go to the ER. The virus just drains you and all you want to do is rest and sleep. I was sleeping close to 20 hours a day and if you know me, I'm lucky to sleep three to four hours a day. Once at the ER, I got out of the car and just told my wife to go home. I had absolutely nothing to say to her because I was so mad that she brought me to the hospital. Once there, I was so uncomfortable. My back was killing me, and I just could not get right with the bed they had in the room. They run all the tests and the doctor comes back and tells me that I had pneumonia and I was septic. I thought okay, can I go home now? That's when he hit me with some logic I needed to hear. He said my kidneys were trying to shut down and he wanted to monitor them to see if my function improved. He said he wasn't going to make me stay but the way things were looking, I could be back in a couple of days to get on dialysis or dead. It was my choice. One of my good friends had just passed away and I had young kids who needed me. I had better let him keep me in the hospital and see how things went. I lie in that bed, unable to sleep. I finally spoke with my wife. I hope I apologized, but knowing my hardheaded self, I probably didn't. I prayed to God that He could see me over this because it seemed when I fell asleep, my whole life would flash before my eyes. What I saw was the times that God kept me from harm or got me out of situations that could have caused me harm or death. From that moment, I had a whole new perspective on life and God had my full attention. When the doctor came in the next day, he told me he wanted to keep me another day, but he knew I wasn't keen on staying any longer than I had to. My kidney function had improved throughout the night. It wasn't where it should be. I was still in stage three kidney disease, but he told me to stay hydrated and get some rest. I knew that was God because I did not want to be on dialysis for the rest of my life. If that happened, I felt that would be the beginning of the end for me, and I know a God who heals. I was refusing to accept that as my fate. I couldn't wait to get home but first they brought me a breakfast tray. When I opened the tray, my cousin Betsy Steele (Pokey) who works in food service at the hospital had sent me a note telling me to get better and that she loved me. Maybe I was vulnerable at that time, but I just broke down crying. She will never know how much that note uplifted my spirits, it just meant so much to me. Pokey, thank you and I love you too!

Once I got home, about five to ten days later, I started to feel better and I went to the doctor and my kidneys had vastly improved from when I was in the hospital and I knew it was God. I still have some things that don't seem right because of Covid and who knows what the disease will do to our bodies in the long run… but I know a God! I finally had my gall bladder surgery about a month later and I was going to prepare to go back to work. The day before I was supposed to go back, I started having what I thought were panic attacks. I thought I was losing my mind. I had been out of work since May because of my gallbladder but Covid delayed everything. It was August and the kids were doing virtual learning, I was taking care of my mother who had dementia and needed 24-7 care and I still didn't feel 100%. Something was just off, and I definitely had to get my mind right, so I extended my short-term disability and sought a mental health counselor. After some tense sessions, it was determined I had PTSD from working in Corrections. Corrections had totally changed me and not for the better. It was starting to go against every moral of my body, and it was just making me deteriorate mentally. After discussions with my wife, counselor and my pastor, it was decided that I was not going back to the Department of Corrections. So, basically in November of 2020, I went on long-term disability and retired from the department. I am still going to counseling to deal with the after-effects of the job I had for 26 years. Throughout the whole time in my career, I realized God covered me and gave me the strength to go in behind those gates every day. God placed my wife where she was in my life through the Covid ordeal. If not, I might not be here to give a testimony of His grace and mercy right now. He has always guided me to where I should be even when I was willfully ignorant to try and do my own thing.

My Message

As my mother would say, I have gone "around Robin Hood's barn" to get to my message. I, for years, practiced a religion that was very foreign to me. Its culture and way of life can be very confusing to someone who grew up a country boy in a Methodist church. I went through the process to show you that the devil will use anything to get you distracted. Whether it is race, politics, false doctrine, work and its employees, even members in the church. The thing is, we are getting mad at the wrong people. My pastor always tells us this. Ephesians 6:12 (KJV) reads "For we wrestle not against flesh and blood, but against principalities, against powers, against the rulers of the darkness of this world, against spiritual wickedness in high places." That means from the outhouse to the White House, we have to fight against these principalities. We are not really fighting against friends but spirits that Satan has put in place to distract you.

I had to live with these obstacles all my life and it has definitely formed the person I am today. I had to go through a process that I would not want anybody who is seeking God the wrong way to go through. The emptiness I felt during those years was overbearing at times. The thing is, during all of the trials and tribulations I have gone through in these few years I have been on this earth, my Lord and Savior has covered me even in all my foolishness. I practiced Islam and I just never felt a connection to God but through those 14 years, He still covered and kept me. Islam is an Abrahamic faith. The difference resides in who Islam believes the area in and around Jerusalem is promised to and the son ship of Jesus Christ. Islam believes that the descendants of Ishmael, Abraham's first son with Hagar was promised the Holy Land instead of Isaac who was Sarai's son. Isaac, the promised child of God to Abraham and Sarai through whom the covenant was established.

In Genesis 16:12, it speaks of Ishmael. "And he will be a wild man; his hand will be against every man, and every man's hand against him; and he shall dwell in the presence of all his brethren." What I gather from this passage is that Ishmael's descendants will be a warring faction. The descendants of Ismael are indeed Muslims. Muslims, Prophet Muhammad according to tradition was a descendant of Ishmael and Abraham. The deity of Jesus is also a problem for me because Islam believes that Jesus was a prophet. They have the utmost respect for Jesus but only believe Him to be a prophet. It states in Galatians 1:8 (KJV), "But though we, or an angel from Heaven, preach any other gospel unto you than that which we have preached unto you, let them be accursed." Once you accept the authority of the Bible as God's Word, you have to take this passage seriously. The Gospel that Paul was referencing was basically Jesus being crucified for the saving of our souls. I know Muslims and others will try to say that there are discrepancies in the Bible through translations and books being discarded from earlier versions but from my personal point of view, there is so much happening in the world that is biblically accurate, I must accept God's Word of the Bible and not an accursed version of the gospel. I know in certain parts of the world it could be a death sentence, but I would implore Muslims who really seek God's face to pray to Him, seek Jesus and He will show Himself to you and give you peace. Jesus is the way, the truth, the light. Seek and serve Him fervently and I know you will enjoy the peace that I have in

Him, no matter what I might be going through.

Conclusion

What you have read is my testimony about living life in two different faiths Abraham. I chose to come back to Christianity because once the Word is revealed to you, you can't deny the truth. God gave me a second chance. He maybe even allowed me to go to another faith for this very reason to give my testimony to Muslims and Christians alike about my journeys with two different cultures who are seeking the same thing but might be a little off on how to reach our heavenly homes and prepare to see His face. We all will meet the Alpha and Omega but how will we present ourselves to someone who knows all? "For it is written, As I live saith the Lord, every knee shall bow to me, and every tongue shall confess to God" (Romans 14:11KJV). The Bible is the only source that if read properly in spirit and with guidance and revelation and a true prayer life can reveal the true and living God. We need to establish a prayer life and talk to God like you would talk to a friend on the phone or sitting right beside you. I implore all Muslims to do just that. Talk with the true and living God. Ask God to reveal Himself to you and if you are wrong about how or who you worship, ask Him to show you the way. I know cultures, separation from family and literal death sentences can persuade you to do otherwise but if you are having doubts, think for just a second because this is your soul we are talking about here. If a death sentence is pronounced on you because of a change in faith to Christianity, I would rather die in Jesus because His name encompasses the total Godhead as noted in scripture. "[6]As ye have therefore received Christ Jesus the Lord, *so* walk ye in him: [7]Rooted and built up in him, and stablished in the faith, as ye have been taught, abounding therein with thanksgiving. [8]Beware lest any man spoil you through philosophy and vain deceit, after the tradition of men, after the rudiments of the world, and not after Christ. [9]For in him dwelleth all the fulness of the Godhead bodily. [10]And ye are complete in him, which is the head of all principality and power: [11]In whom also ye are circumcised with the circumcision made without hands, in putting off the body of the sins of the flesh by the circumcision of Christ: [12]Buried with him in baptism, wherein also ye are risen with *him* through the faith of the operation of God, who hath raised him from the dead" (Colossians 2:6-12). He alone is the Father, Son and Holy Spirit all wrapped in one Jesus. Many prophets have spoken of His coming and I can tell you that He is coming back and we all will bow down to Him. You just have to look at the state of the world now. The signs are there, it won't be long. Get your life in order because He has shut down our way of life with the Coronavirus. We can't go to church like we used to, businesses are shut down. There is no excuse, He should have your undivided attention. Now is the time. If you don't have a prayer life, GET ONE! I am not a prophet, but I can say that with as much confidence as I have ever had. Jesus is the only way. You don't need a mediator, priest or Pope to speak for you. Go to Him in prayer and I can assure you He will run to you and reveal Himself. He is not going to promise you an easy road but know that once you repent, be baptized in Jesus' name, you WILL receive the gift of the Holy Ghost and you WILL have a permanent guide and counsellor through life to help you with the road you are going to travel on.

I pray that this memoir of my life and struggles will help you come to a better understanding in Jesus, maybe strengthen your faith or just give you something entertaining and positive to read. I told you I have God dwelling with me through the Holy Ghost. Something I haven't told you is that it costs you. Not money but your service and time to the true and living God. God has told me to write this memoir and get my testimony out to the masses. I personally believe He interrupted my sleep and everything else I wanted to do because I have not followed His instructions. I finally submitted to His will and wrote this memoir. It was actually good for me to write this memoir and tell my journey because I would hope no one else would have to go through the stuff I went through just to come back to something that I was already aware of. I just had to go through life and do things a little harder to accomplish what I wanted because I went against the grain which was God's will. I plan on doing seminars and I am sure maybe biblical scholars or Quranic scholars might attack me, but I will say this up front. I will not argue about it, but I will just tell you about the goodness of God and how good He has been to me even through all my mess. I will end this with peace be unto you! May God bless you and may you love our Lord and Savior, Jesus Christ, like never before.

Dedication

This book is dedicated to my wife who has stuck with me through thick and thin. You are always there encouraging me to do things I never thought possible. Now it is my turn to push you to heights you never thought you could reach. I love you to life, my love!

Acknowledgements

First and foremost, I would like to thank my Lord and Savior Jesus Christ! He has let me experience a heck of a ride but gave me His comforter to rely on and I know without You I would not have completed or even attempted this memoir. This, all for Your glory, all praise belongs to Him. I would like to thank my lovely wife, Denise Rashad, who has listened to me talk about the memoir but never saw me do anything for years. She probably thought I was full of crap and just talked about it but would never get started. Thank you, my love, for reading so many revisions and encouraging me to do what God told me to do. I love you! I would like to thank Elder Lance Turner for calling the fact that I had not started on my book "a shame!" You just don't know but what you said to me that day got my competitive juices flowing and I took it as a challenge so thank you for getting me to finally get up off my shoulders and write this memoir. I want to thank Deja Braxton, author of the book "Dear Ezra" who poured over my book and tried probably in vain to correct my grammar. Deja, I know you probably thought "does this dude really have a degree?" but I assure you I struggled in college also. Thank you for your remarks, comments and red/blue ink on this project. They are most assuredly appreciated young lady. Thank you to my cousin/big brother Mike Miller aka Melvin for your support. You always have a way of supporting me and lecturing me whether I want it or not. I know you don't think I listen to you but in reality I hear every Word you say but I just might not like it. Thank you for being real bruh, I love you bruh but if you tell anybody, I will cut your big toe off! I would like to thank my mom, Barbara (Jenny) Steele, for always being there for me and encouraging me in my endeavors. To my grandmother, Anna Steele, and my uncle, Captain Gregory B Steele, I miss y'all like crazy and wish you were here to see some of the things I have accomplished because I have you two in mind when I attempt to do anything. I want to send shout outs to my aunt, Karen Steele, and my cousins, Gregory and Jeremy. I love y'all with all my heart and never forget it. To my cousin, Betty Russell, Roger Gilbert, and that tribe of kids of Betty's, Ashley, Alesha, Amber and Austin, I just want y'all to know I love each and every one of y'all! Shout out to Bishop Nolan Wolfe, First Lady Alicia Wolfe and everybody at Antioch

Greater Love Ministries. I love each and every one of y'all and just keep doing what y'all do, keep praising! If you want to praise God and have fun doing it, come to Antioch Greater Love Ministries. They are radical for God! To two of my biggest inspirations to even get up sometimes when I just don't feel like doing nothing, my boys Trayvon and Tyrese. Y'all are so lively and spoiled but you have such a sweet spirit. I hope that God uses you in ways that I could never imagine. I pray to see it and I pray you will not be as hard-headed with the direction of God as your daddy was. I love you two so much and want nothing but the best for you both. I know I may seem hard on you two at times but that is because I know this world can be cruel at times and Daddy has seen some crazy stuff. I just want you to be prepared for what life can throw at you and know that with Jesus on your side, you will be able to get through it. You both have been baptized in Jesus' name, next y'all have to get the Holy Ghost and I know you will be prepared for life. Follow God, young men, just follow God. With Him you can't go wrong. Love you two terrorists! If I have by chance left anyone off of here, please blame the head not the heart. It's not that I don't have love for you, it's just I'm forgetful and it gets worse as I get older so please forgive me.

Thanks to whoever reads this memoir. I hope you enjoyed it as much as I did writing it. I pray it was informative and gave you insight into why folks are searching for God. Please teach in Bible schools and wherever you can to promote the name of Jesus because people are searching and all they are receiving is vain philosophy. Give them the true Word of God, the unadulterated truth. No matter how much it hurts, let people know the truth. We need it in this world we live in! Thank you again and God bless!

About the Author

Gregory Alexander Stanback was born March 11, 1972, to the late Floyd Benjamin Stanback and Barbara Anna Steele. Greg was influenced in his early years by his maternal grandmother, Anna Steele, and his uncle, Gregory B. Steele, Jr., aka Bubba. Greg graduated from Marion Senior High School in 1990 and attended Clinch Valley College, now known as The University of Virginia at Wise. He lost his scholarship after two years and eventually went to Wytheville Community College but still did not graduate. He thought it best just to enter the work force because he didn't believe school was for him. He started working for the Virginia Department of Corrections on July 12, 1994 at Powhatan State prison. A year later, he transferred to James River Correctional Center and in 1998. Due to his mother's health concerns, he transferred to Marion Correctional Treatment Center where he retired as a Lieutenant in 2020 after 26 years of service. He changed his name in 1997 to

Gregory Alexander Abdullah Rashad legally and does not like to be called by his given name, Stanback, due to his father's absence in his life. He finally earned his Bachelor of Science degree in Criminal Justice from Bluefield College in 2008. He started working on his Master's degree in Criminal Justice at Radford University in 2008 but took a break from the course work because of family obligations at the time. He intends to return at some point for his Master's degree soon. Gregory is a Freemason, and his lodge is Mt. Pleasant Lodge #31 where he currently serves as Past Master/Senior Warden and Assistant District Deputy for the 20th Masonic District. He has also attained his 32nd degree at Acorn Consistory in The Valley of Roanoke in Roanoke Virginia. He also is a member of Tri Community Chapter of the Eastern Star where his wife, Denise, is a member also. Greg and his family attend Antioch Greater Love Ministries in Marion Virginia where he is currently a deacon. Greg also works with Turks food pantry named after his late aunt, Elizabeth "Turk" White. The service is used as an emergency service for people in need until they may receive help from bigger food pantries in the area. Greg currently resides in Marion, Virginia with his wife, Denise, and his two twin sons, Trayvon and Tyrese.

9 7 9 8 7 1 2 6 7 6 3 2 3